Go to **www.ketoveo.com** for more guides and resources to help
you on your keto journey.

42 GREAT BRITISH KETO RECIPES

Contents

TEA TIME

DESSERTS

Notes:

Salt should be sea salt or pink Himalayan salt.

Use organic foods as much as possible.

Coconut oil should be 100% unrefined, virgin, and raw.

Baking Powder should be aluminum free.

Baking powder should be gluten-free and aluminum-free.

HISTORY OF BRITISH CUISINE

The United Kingdom comprises Ireland, Wales, Scotland and England and each of them has a rich culture with divers culinary traditions.

About 4000 BC, domestic animals were brought from the mainland to the British Isles such as cattle, pigs and sheep.

In the first century AD, Rome began their conquest of the isles. Romans where experienced road builders which made it possible to easily transport people and goods far and wide. They imported pheasants, rabbits, brown hare, nuts, cherries, peas, corn, spices and herbs such as garlic, pepper, thyme and basil and also wine.

After 400 years of rule, the Romans occupying forces began to abandon the British Isles to fight wars elsewhere in their empire. This left the isles open for conquest from groups. Germanic tribes of people from northern Germany and Scandinavia; the Jutes, Angles and the Saxons then conquered the isles. The culture that developed over the next few hundred years, called Anglo-Saxon, was the impetus for the English language and culture that exists in the British isles today. These people were skilled in hunting and farming as well as cultivating a wide variety of herbs which influenced the tradition of cooking in Britain as well.

From 800 to 1100 AD, the Vikings raided and traded in the area and brought techniques for smoking and drying fish and meats. They were greatly advanced with their cooking skills and their dishware were well-designed and crafted. Many Vikings even settled in the north-east of Britain and a few rose not only to positions of prominence and power, Britain had kings of Viking descent.

The Trifle, a traditional British dessert, was first mentioned in 1585 in an English cookbook *The Good Huswifes Jewell*.

Starting in the late 17th century and continuing well into the 19th century, pepper and fine spices such as saffron were imported and had a tremendous impact on British cuisine. Indian dishes became especially popular.

One famous British food is the Yorkshire Pudding. It has been suggested that the pudding got the name 'Yorkshire' due to the region's association with coal and the higher temperatures this produced which helped to make the batter crispier. 1737, a recipe for "a dripping pudding" was published in the book *The Whole Duty of a Woman*.

And of course everyone knows what a sandwich is. This legendary item of food as we know it was popularized in England in 1762 by John Montagu, the 4th Earl of Sandwich. He was a British statesman and a notorious gambler. Legend has it that rather than leave the card table to have his dinner, he ordered his valet to bring him slices of meat between two slices of bread so he could continue his gambling non-stop.

In 1847 Joseph Fry discovered how to make a chocolate bar proper for consumption. And about 1860 the well-known Fish and Chips was invented though the true source is unclear. Fish and chips is one of the most popular meals in Britain; even Charles Dickens, the famous British writer makes mention of them in two of his books.

Steak & kidney pie, Christmas dinner, the Sunday roast, shepherd's pie, as well are belong also to the traditional British foods.

MAIN DISHES

BANGERS AND MASH

Servings: 4

Nutritional Facts Per Serving:

Carbs:	6 g	Protein:	15 g
Fatss:	31 g	Calories:	378 kcal

INGREDIENTS

Bangers:

4 sausages

1 cup sliced raw onions

1 tbsp coconut oil

1 tbsp butter

½ cup chicken stock

salt and pepper

Mash:

1 head of cauliflower

2 tbsp heavy cream

1 tbsp butter

2 oz Dubliner or other sharp cheese

salt and pepper to taste

2 tbsp chopped parsley

This is how you make the recipe

1. Bangers: Cook the sausages in a saute pan until browned and cooked through. Remove them from the pan.

2. Cook onions, along with the butter and coconut oil until onions are browned and softened.

3. Add chicken stock and cook for another 3 – 5 minutes. Add heavy cream and stir slowly for a minute. Season with salt and pepper.

4. Place the sausages in the pan with the onions for a few more minutes.

5. Mash: Clean and trim the cauliflower, breaking it into medium sized pieces.

6. Steam the cauliflower until tender, about 10 - 15 minutes.

7. Place it into a high speed blender or food processor along with the cream, butter and cheese. Puree until smooth.

8. Season with salt and pepper to taste. You can adjust the cream and butter to your preference.

9. Place ½ cup of cauliflower mash and one sausage to each plate and top with onion gravy.

10. Garnish with chopped parsley.

BUBBLE AND SQUEAK MINI FRITTATAS

Servings: 6			
Nutritional Facts Per Serving:			
Carbs:	8.4 g	Protein:	27.9 g
Fatss:	25.2 g	Calories:	368 kcal

This is a traditional English dish which was originally created to use up leftovers. The main ingredients were made from boiled potatoes and cabbage. Later, Brussels sprouts and vegetables were added. The earliest-known recipe was in Mrs Rundell's: A New System of Domestic Cookery, in 1806. The name comes from the bubbling and squeaking noises the mixture makes in the hot oil while being fried.

INGREDIENTS

10 eggs
1 cup leftover roast lamb (or other leftover roast meat, such as chicken, beef or turkey)
1 cup cooked veggies (pumpkin, broccoli, carrot or other leftover vegetables), cut into cubes
1½ cups cabbage, kale, Brussels sprouts or other leftover greens, shredded
½ cup coconut cream
3 tbsp coconut oil or ghee
1 large red onion, diced
2 garlic cloves, crushed
2 tbsp chopped parsley
salt and pepper o taste

This is how you make the recipe

1. Preheat the oven to 350°F and prepare a baking tray with parchment paper.

2. In a bowl, whisk the eggs lightly with the coconut cream and season well with salt and pepper. Set aside.

3. Heat the coconut oil or ghee. Add the onion and garlic, cook for 3-5 minutes until soft and slightly golden. Stir in the leftover meat, vegetables and parsley and cook slowly for 2-3 minutes. Season with salt and pepper, transfer to the prepared tray, then pour in the egg mixture. Mix slightly.

4. Place in the oven and bake for 30 minutes or until golden on top and the eggs are cooked.

5. Leave the frittatas to cool for 5 minutes. Cut into portions and serve.

CASSEROLE

Servings: 6			
Nutritional Facts Per Serving:			
Carbs:	3.1 g	Protein:	16.6 g
Fats:	28.4 g	Calories:	334 kcal

INGREDIENTS

1 head cauliflower

3 oz butter

½ tsp salt

½ tsp pepper

½ lb bacon, sliced into strips

⅔ cup parmesan cheese, shredded

⅓ cup Mozzarella cheese, shredded

This is how you make the recipe

1. Preheat oven to 390°F.

2. Boil a pot of water and add the cauliflower, cook for 5-8 minutes until the cauliflower is tender.

3. Remove the cauliflower, drain the pot and then return it to the warm pot. Add the butter, salt and pepper.

4. Blend with a immersion blender until the cauliflower is a smooth puree. Set aside

5. In a frying pan, sauté the bacon until crispy.

6. Add most of the bacon grease into the cauliflower puree.

7. Add half of the parmesan cheese into the cauliflower puree and mix well.

8. Pour the cauliflower mixture into a casserole dish.

9. Top with the remaining bacon, parmesan cheese, and mozzarella cheese.

10. Bake in the oven for 20 minutes, until the cheese is melted and browning.

11. Remove from the oven and serve.

GREATEST BRITISH KETO RECIPES

CORNISH PASTIES DELUXE

Servings: 8

Nutritional Facts Per Serving:
Carbs: 6.7 g Protein: 20.6 g
Fats: 48 g Calories: 550 kcal

INGREDIENTS

Crust:

7 oz almond flour

3 oz coconut flour

1 tsp xanthan gum

½ tsp salt

8 oz butter, cold

8 oz cream cheese, cold

2 eggs, lightly beaten

4 tsp apple cider vinegar

Filling:

1 lb ground beef

7 oz rutabaga, diced small

3½ oz carrots, diced small

¼ of a large onion

salt and pepper to taste

oat fiber

This is how you make the recipe

1. Place almond flour, coconut flour, xanthan gum and salt in a food processor and pulse to combine.

2. Add butter and pulse until it resembles coarse crumbs.

3. Add cream cheese and pulse again until it looks like wet sand.

4. Add eggs and vinegar and pulse just until incorporated.

5. Place the dough onto a sheet of cling wrap and flatten it into a disc for easier handling.

6. Enclose it tightly in cling wrap and refrigerate for at least an hour, or overnight.

7. Pre-heat the oven to 375˚F.

8. Mix chopped veggies with beef, and season with salt and pepper.

9. Divide the filling into 8 equal pieces.

10. Shape each piece into a ball.

11. Place a ball onto a sheet of parchment paper which has been liberally sprinkled with oat fiber. Sprinkle more oat fiber on top, then place another piece of parchment paper on top.

12. With a wooden roller, roll the dough between the two sheets of parchment paper to ⅛ inch thickness, in the shape of an oval.

13. Peel off top piece of parchment paper.

14. Place ⅛ of the filling on one half of the oval, then use the parchment paper to fold the dough over the filling.

15. Crimp edges. Trim off excess parchment paper and place on baking sheets. (You'll need two to bake all 8 at once.) Repeat for each piece of dough. Place in the refrigerator for 10 minutes before baking.

16. Bake for 45-55 minutes, or until outside is golden and inside has reached 170˚F. If they start to brown too quickly, cover with foil for the rest of the baking time.

CORNISH PASTIES

Servings: 4		
Nutritional Facts Per Serving:		
Carbs: 17.8 g	Protein:	89 g
Fats: 69 g	Calories:	729 kcal

INGREDIENTS

Pasty Filling:

1 tbsp coconut oil

12 oz beef skirt steak, finely diced

1 large red onion, finely diced

6 oz rutabaga, fincly diced

6 oz carrots, finely diced

1 pint beef stock

salt and pepper to taste

"Fat-Head" Dough:

6 oz grated mozzarella

3 oz almond flour

2 tbsp full-fat cream cheese

1 egg

1 tsp onion flakes

salt

This is how you make the recipe

1. Filling: Fry the onion in the coconut oil until it is transparent.

2. Add the beef to the onion and brown the meat.

3. Now include the rest of the vegetables and leave it on a low heat with a lid for 5 minutes to allow all ingredients to begin cooking and for flavors to combine.

4. Pour over the beef stock, so that it almost but not fully covers the mixture, and bring it to a boil.

5. Season with salt and pepper, then turn down the heat and simmer for 30 minutes.

6. Strain all liquid and set aside for later.

7. Dough: In a bowl, thoroughly mix together the almond flour, grated mozzarella and cream cheese.

8. Put the bowl on a warm place, until the cheeses begin to melt.

9. Add the egg, salt and onion flakes and give the mix a really good stir.

10. Pre-heat oven to 425°F.

11. To roll out; divide the mixture into four parts and then roll each separately using a rolling pin, between 2 sheets of parchment paper into rough round shapes about 6 inches in diameter.

12. Top each with a spoonful of meat filling and fold in half; pinch to seal and brush with a beaten egg. Make slits in the top and bake until golden, about 15 minutes.

COTTAGE PIE

Servings: 6			
Nutritional Facts Per Serving:			
Carbs:	8 g	Protein:	18 g
Fats:	36 g	Calories:	420 kcal

The name "cottage pie" was first used at the end of the 18th century. It was around that time that the poorer people of Britain, people who lived in cottages in the country, started using potatoes as an everyday food. Originally, a pie made with any kind of meat and mashed potato was called a "cottage pie". In modern British English, the dish is usually called "cottage pie" if it is made with beef. If it is made with lamb it is usually called "shepherd's pie".

INGREDIENTS

2 lb ground beef
1 cup beef stock
1 large head of cauliflower, cut into evenly sized florets
1 small onion, diced
3 sticks celery, diced
3 oz butter
3 egg yolks
2 cloves garlic, crushed
¼ cup red wine vinegar
3 tbsp tomato paste
3 tbsp coconut oil
2 tbsp fresh thyme
1 tbsp dried oregano
1 tsp salt
¼ tsp pepper
a pinch of paprika
a pinch of dried oregano

This is how you make the recipe

1. In coconut oil, place the garlic, oregano, onion and celery and saute for 5 minutes, until the onion is starting to become translucent.

2. Add the salt and ground beef, stirring continuously to break apart the meat while it browns.

3. When the beef is browned, add the tomato paste and stir well.

4. Add the beef stock and red wine vinegar and simmer uncovered for 20 minutes until the liquid has reduced. Add the thyme.

5. Spoon the beef mixture into your casserole dish and set aside.

6. Preheat your oven to 350°F.

7. Fill a large saucepan ⅔ full of water and bring it to a boil.

8. Add the cauliflower and cook for 7-10 minutes until tender.

9. Pour the water and cauliflower into a colander and drain well.

10. Return the drained cauliflower to the saucepan, along with the butter, salt and pepper.

11. Using your immersion blender, blend the cauliflower into a smooth mash.

12. Add the egg yolks and blend well.

13. Gently spoon the mashed cauliflower onto the beef mixture into your casserole dish.

14. Sprinkle with paprika and oregano.

15. Bake the pie in the oven for 25-30 minutes, until the mash is golden brown.

COTTAGE PIE WITH CAULIFLOWER MASH

Servings: 4

Nutritional Facts Per Serving:
Carbs: 20.1 g   Protein: 43.6 g
Fats: 28.4 g   Calories: 507 kcal

INGREDIENTS

1 lb ground beef

4 tomatoes, diced

1 cauliflower head, cut into florets

1 large carrot, diced

1 celery stick, diced

1 onion, diced

1 tsp thyme

2 cups vegetable broth

3 oz tomato paste

2 tbsp Worcestershire sauce

½ stick butter

2 garlic cloves, minced

½ cup heavy cream

⅓ cup shredded cheese

salt and pepper to taste

This is how you make the recipe

1. Preheat oven to 350°F.

2. Brown the ground beef in a pan at medium-high heat.

3. Add the onion, tomato, carrot, celery, thyme, vegetable broth, tomato paste, Worcestershire sauce and cook until the veggies are soft and the sauce thickens.

4. While the ground beef cooks, boil a pot of water and cook the cauliflower florets for 10 minutes.

5. Melt the butter together with the garlic in a small pan.

6. Once the cauliflower is cooked, toss it into a food processor and add the butter, garlic and cream.

7. Blend until smooth and season with salt and pepper.

8. Then stir ½ cup of cheese into the mash until it's melted.

9. Divide the ground beef equally into four 8 oz ramekins and top with the cauliflower mash.

10. Sprinkle remaining cheese on top of the cauliflower mash.

11. Bake for 20 minutes and under the broiler for about 5 minutes.

12. Remove and garnish with roughly chopped parsley.

FISH PIE

Servings: 4

Nutritional Facts Per Serving:

Carbs:	3.7 g	Protein:	45 g
Fats:	45 g	Calories:	621 kcal

INGREDIENTS

10 oz fish pie mix chunks (salmon, smoked haddock, Atlantic cod)

9 oz raw peeled jumbo king prawns

3 anchovies

4 cups frozen cauliflower florets

2 large eggs

1 garlic clove

⅓ cup double cream (heavy cream)

¼ cup cheddar cheese

4 oz coarse salt

2 oz butter

1 tbsp capers

1 tbsp broth granules

½ cup fresh parsley

¼ tsp ground pepper

⅛ tsp fine salt

¼ tsp nutmeg

This is how you make the recipe

1. Place cauliflower florets in a large pan, fill with enough water so as to submerge.

2. Add the coarse salt and bring to a boil, then simmer until tender (3-5 minutes).

3. Drain florets and put them back into the pan with nutmeg, 1½ tbsp butter and 2 tbsp cream.

4. Stir, then blend until smooth, set aside to cool.

5. Once cool, fold in grated cheddar and leave for later.

6. Peel and mince the garlic clove, and put it in a medium frying pan with 3 tbsp butter and anchovies.

7. Fry over medium-high heat for 1 minute.

8. Add prawns, fine salt, pepper and broth granules, cook with lid on until pink (4-5 minutes), stirring a couple of times.

9. Meanwhile, bring a small pot of water to a boil, lower eggs into it and set the timer for 6 minutes.

10. Back to the frying pan, add mixed fish chunks, capers and 3½ tbsp cream, and cook with lid on for a further 3 minutes.

11. Again, stir carefully to ensure even cooking but don't overdo it or the fish chunks will break up and turn to mush.

12. Finally, add chopped parsley and leave to cool a little with lid off.

13. Peel and cut each egg into quarters placing them directly into your pie dish.

14. Scoop the fish mix over the eggs.

15. Spoon cauliflower mash over the fish and grill (broil) for 10-15 minutes until you see golden brown peaks on top.

BEEF CHEESE PIE

Servings: 7

Nutritional Facts Per Serving:

Carbs:	14.8 g	Protein:	28.7 g
Fats:	37.5 g	Calories:	503 kcal

INGREDIENTS

Filling:

1¼ lb ground beef (or ground lamb to make a Lamb Cheese Pie)

½ yellow onion, finely chopped

4 tbsp tomato paste, pesto or ajvar relish

2 tbsp butter or coconut oil

1 garlic clove, finely chopped

1 tbsp dried oregano or dried basil

½ cup water

salt and pepper to taste

Pie crust:

¾ cup almond flour

4 tbsp sesame seeds

4 tbsp coconut flour

1 tbsp psyllium husk powder

1 tsp baking powder

3 tbsp coconut oil

1 egg

4 tbsp water

a pinch of salt

Topping:

8 oz cottage cheese

8 oz shredded cheese

This is how you make the recipe

1. Preheat the oven to 350°F.

2. Fry onion and garlic in butter or coconut oil over medium heat for a few minutes, until the onion is soft. Add the ground meat and continue frying. Add oregano or basil and add salt and pepper to taste.

3. Add tomato paste, pesto or ajvar relish, whichever you have to hand. Add water. Lower the heat and let simmer for at least 20 minutes. While the meat simmers, make the dough for the crust.

4. Mix all the dough ingredients in a food processor for a few minutes until the dough turns into a ball. If you don't have a food processor, you can mix by hand with a fork.

5. Place a round piece of parchment paper in a well-greased 9-10 inch spring-form pan to make it easier to remove the pie when it's done. (You can also use a deep-dish pie pan.) Spread the dough in the pan and up along the sides. Use a spatula or well-greased fingers.

6. Pre-bake the crust for 10-15 minutes. Take it out of the oven and place the meat in the crust.

7. Mix cottage cheese and shredded cheese together, and layer on top of the pie.

8. Bake for 30-40 minutes on lower rack or until the pie has turned a golden color.

9. Serve with a fresh green salad and dressing.

PORK CHEESE PIE

Servings: 7			
Nutritional Facts Per Serving:			
Carbs:	14.8 g	Protein:	65.1 g
Fats:	37.3 g	Calories:	656 kcal

INGREDIENTS

Filling:

1¼ lb ground pork

½ yellow onion, finely chopped

4 tbsp tomato paste, pesto or ajvar relish

2 tbsp butter or coconut oil

1 garlic clove, finely chopped

1 tbsp dried oregano or dried basil

½ cup water

salt and pepper to taste

Pie crust:

¾ cup almond flour

4 tbsp sesame seeds

4 tbsp coconut flour

1 tbsp psyllium husk powder

1 tsp baking powder

3 tbsp coconut oil

1 egg

4 tbsp water

a pinch of salt

Topping:

8 oz cottage cheese

8 oz shredded cheese

This is how you make the recipe

1. Preheat the oven to 350°F.

2. Fry onion and garlic in butter or coconut oil over medium heat for a few minutes, until the onion is soft. Add the ground pork and continue frying. Add oregano or basil and add salt and pepper to taste.

3. Add tomato paste, pesto or ajvar relish, whichever you have to hand. Add water. Lower the heat and let simmer for at least 20 minutes. While the meat simmers, make the dough for the crust.

4. Mix all the dough ingredients in a food processor for a few minutes until the dough turns into a ball. If you don't have a food processor, you can mix by hand with a fork.

5. Place a round piece of parchment paper in a well-greased 9-10 inch spring-form pan to make it easier to remove the pie when it's done. (You can also use a deep-dish pie pan.) Spread the dough in the pan and up along the sides. Use a spatula or well-greased fingers.

6. Pre-bake the crust for 10-15 minutes. Take it out of the oven and place the meat in the crust.

7. Mix cottage cheese and shredded cheese together, and layer on top of the pie.

8. Bake for 30-40 minutes on lower rack or until the pie has turned a golden color.

9. Serve with a fresh green salad and dressing.

PORK PIE

Servings: 4			
Nutritional Facts Per Serving:			
Carbs:	5 g	Protein:	30.4 g
Fats:	43.1 g	Calories:	559 kcal

INGREDIENTS

Filling:

1 lb ground pork
4 tbsp grated parmesan cheese
2 large eggs, beaten
½ tsp ground nutmeg
½ tsp ginger
½ tsp cardamom
zest of ½ lemon
salt and pepper to taste

Pie crust:

3/4 cup almond flour
3 tbsp sesame seeds
2 oz coconut flour
1½ tbsp ground psyllium husk powder
1½ tsp baking powder
3 tbsp coconut oil
1 egg
2 oz water
salt to taste

This is how you make the recipe

1. Add meat and spices to a pan over medium-high heat. Once slightly cooked, remove from heat and add egg and lemon zest.

2. Mix all the dough ingredients in a food processor for a few minutes until the dough turns into a ball. If you don't have a food processor, you can mix by hand with a fork.

3. Place a round piece of parchment paper in a well-greased 9-10 inch spring-form pan to make it easier to remove the pie when it's done. (You can also use a deep-dish pie pan.) Spread the dough in the pan and up along the sides. Use a spatula or well-greased fingers.

4. Pre-bake the crust for 10-15 minutes.

5. Spoon mixture into pie shells and bake at 350°F for 20-25 minutes in the oven.

6. Remove from oven, let cool, and serve.

BRITISH STYLE BUFFALO CHICKEN EMPANADAS

Servings: 12

Nutritional Facts Per Serving:
Carbs: 4.6 g Protein: 28.8 g
Fats: 33.7 g Calories: 437 kcal

Empanadas are popular in Britain as they are quite similar to, but more spicy than pasties. The filling is made of shredded chicken. You can try different filling types that you like. We season chicken with butter and hot sauce.

INGREDIENTS

Empanada dough:
1½ cup mozzarella cheese
3 oz cream cheese
2 cups almond flour
1 egg

Buffalo Chicken Filling:
2 cups shredded chicken, cooked
⅓ cup hot sauce
2 tbsp butter, melted

This is how you make the recipe

1. Prepare the oven and preheat it to 425°F.

2. Warm the mozzarella with the cream cheese, mix them and then stir.

3. Afterwards, reheat for one more minute and stir to combine the mixture thoroughly.

4. Whisk the egg, then pour it with the almond flour into the cheese mixture. Stir well.

5. Keep adding more almond flour as needed until the mixture does not stick to your fingers anymore. Set aside for later.

6. In a separate bowl, pour the hot sauce and butter over the shredded chicken. Mix thoroughly until the chicken is entirely covered in sauce.

7. Lay some plastic wrap or parchment paper on a flat surface. Dust with almond flour so the dough will not stick.

8. Likewise, grease the rolling pin with some coconut oil. Flatten the dough into ¼ inch thickness.

9. Cut circles from the dough approx. 4 inches in diameter. Gather the excess dough, roll it out once more and repeat the process until all the dough has been cut into circles.

10. On each circle, put a spoonful of chicken onto one side. Fold the other half over the filling.

11. Press the edges of the dough firmly so the filling is tightly enclosed. Slightly roll the edges to ensure that the fillings will not spill out.

12. Arrange the empanadas on a cooking sheet greased with some oil. Bake for 8-10 minutes.

13. Remove from the oven once the dough turns golden brown in color. Transfer to a plate and top with some chopped chives if preferred. Enjoy.

FISH AND CHIPS

Servings: 6

Nutritional Facts Per Serving:

Carbs:	6 g	Protein:	57 g
Fats:	86 g	Calories:	1092 kcal

INGREDIENTS

Tartar sauce:

¾ cup keto-friendly mayonnaise

4 tbsp dill pickle relish

½ tbsp curry powder

Chips:

1½ lb rutabaga

1 tbsp coconut oil

salt and pepper to taste

Fish:

1½ lb white fish

2 eggs

1 cup almond flour

1 cup grated parmesan cheese

1 tsp paprika powder

½ tsp onion powder

1 tsp salt

¼ tsp pepper

2 cups beef tallow, or organic lard, for frying

This is how you make the recipe

1. Mix all ingredients for the tartar sauce. Place in the refrigerator while making the rest of the dish.

2. Preheat the oven to 400°F. Peel the rutabaga and cut into chips (thin sticks about ¼ - ⅜ inch wide). Brush the chips with oil and place on a baking sheet lined with parchment paper.

3. Sprinkle with salt and pepper.

4. Bake in the oven for about 30 minutes, depending on the thickness of the chips, until golden brown.

5. In the meantime, prepare the fish. Crack the eggs in a bowl and use a fork to combine.

6. On a plate, mix almond flour, parmesan cheese and seasonings.

7. Cut the fish in bite-sized pieces, approximately 1 x 1 inch, and cover with the flour mix. Dip in beaten eggs and then cover again with flour.

8. Heat the tallow or lard in a deep sauce pan to 340°-360°F. You can also use a deep fryer if you have one, follow instructions for your device.

9. Fry the fish for 3 minutes on each side or until the breading is golden brown and the fish is cooked through.

10. Serve with the baked rutabaga chips and tartar sauce.

SWANKY FISH AND CHIPS

Servings: 6			
Nutritional Facts Per Serving:			
Carbs:	6 g	Protein:	42 g
Fats:	60 g	Calories:	743 kcal

INGREDIENTS

2 lb skinless firm white fish fillets

2 eggs

2 avocados

2 large zucchini, cut into long wedges

1 tbsp pouring cream

1½ cups almond meal

½ cup finely grated parmesan cheese

zest of 1 large lemon

⅓ cup finely chopped fresh parsley

1 tsp chili flakes

⅓ cup organic lard

mixed salad leaves, to serve

lemon wedges, to serve

This is how you make the recipe

1. Preheat oven to 400°F.

2. Line a large baking tray with parchment paper.

3. Whisk the eggs, cream and 1 tbsp water together in a large shallow bowl.

4. Combine the almond meal, cheese, zest, parsley and chili flakes (if using) in a shallow bowl.

5. Halve each avocado, remove stone, peel away skin and cut each into 6-8 wedges.

6. Working one piece at a time, coat a piece of avocado in the egg mixture, allowing excess to drip off, then coat in the almond meal mixture. Repeat with the remaining avocado, the zucchini and the fish.

7. Spread the avocado and zucchini evenly over prepared tray. Place fish on a plate, cover and place in the refrigerator for 10 minutes to rest.

8. Spray the avocado and zucchini generously with oil. Bake for 20 minutes or until golden and crisp.

9. Heat the lard in a large non-stick frying pan over medium-high heat and cook the fish for 2-3 minutes each side or until golden and crisp.

10. Serve fish and chips with salad leaves and lemon wedges.

BACON AND EGG BREAKFAST WRAPS WITH AVOCADO

Servings: 4

Nutritional Facts Per Serving:

Carbs:	4 g	Protein:	27 g
Fats:	38 g	Calories:	469 kcal

INGREDIENTS

"Almost zero carb" wraps:

4 oz plain pork rinds, crushed

⅛ tsp baking soda

¼ tsp salt, optional

4 oz cream cheese, softened

6 eggs

½ cup water

Coconut oil, for griddle

Bacon and eggs:

12 slices bacon, cooked

8 large eggs

2 cups grated cheddar cheese

2 avocados, sliced

1 cup salsa

salt and pepper to taste

This is how you make the recipe

1. Wraps: Place the pork rinds in a food processor and process until they become a fine powder.

2. Add the baking soda and salt and give it a little pulse to mix.

3. Add the eggs and cheese and process until smooth and thick.

4. Add the water and blend until all of the ingredients are completely incorporated.

5. Pour into a bowl and let sit for 5-10 minutes until the batter thickens to the consistency of cream of wheat.

6. Preheat a pancake griddle over medium heat. When hot, oil the griddle and then gently wipe-off the excess with a paper towel.

7. Using a ¼ cup measure, pour the batter onto the skillet and spread into a 5 inch circle with the back of a spoon. Make it as thin as possible. I dip my spoon in water to prevent it from sticking to the batter. Cook like you would a pancake. NOTE: You will need to thin the batter as it sits. Add 1 tbsp of water at a time as needed.

8. Keep in the refrigerator up to a week or freeze with a piece of waxed paper between each wrap.

9. Bacon and eggs: Cook the bacon in a pan until crisp.

10. Remove, cut in half and set aside.

11. Pour out all but 2 tsp of bacon fat. Slice the avocado.

12. In a bowl, beat the eggs and half of the cheddar cheese.

13. Cook the scrambled eggs to your liking and remove from the pan. Season with salt and pepper.

14. Place the wraps into the hot pan over medium heat.

15. Divide the scrambled eggs and place them on ½ of each wrap, not going past the middle. Add the avocado, bacon and remaining cheese.

16. Add 1 tbsp of water to the pan and cover quickly with a lid. Leave covered for 1-2 minutes or until the cheese has melted and the bottom of the wraps have browned a bit. Serve with salsa.

FISH AND CHIPS DELUXE

Servings: 2

Nutritional Facts Per Serving:

Carbs:	1 g	Protein:	26 g
Fats:	13 g	Calories:	242 kcal

INGREDIENTS

Fish:

9 oz firm white fish, preferably Atlantic cod

⅓ cup sour cream

1 egg

1 tbsp sour cream or coconut cream

2 tsp apple cider vinegar

4 cloves of garlic, pressed

1 tsp baking powder

½ cup whey protein isolate

¼ tsp garlic powder

avocado oil or oil of choice

salt to taste

Chips:

1 medium jicama, peeled and cut into slices about ¼ inch thick (about 4-5 cups)

1 tbsp avocado oil

½ tsp turmeric

½ tsp garlic powder

½ tsp onion powder

½ tsp sea salt

¼ tsp black pepper

This is how you make the recipe

1. Fish: Mix sour cream or coconut cream with the vinegar, garlic and season to taste with salt.

2. Cut the fish across the grain of the flesh into strips approx. two inches wide, and add them to the cream marinade. Cover and refrigerate for two hours, preferably overnight.

3. Prepare your frying station by adding enough oil to a skillet or pan to make it about ½-inch deep. You can save a lot of oil by using a narrower pan and frying in batches. Heat up oil over medium-low heat while you coat the fish.

4. Mix the whey protein, baking powder, garlic powder and salt in a shallow plate or dish.

5. In a second plate or dish, whisk the egg with cream and vinegar.

6. Coat the fish by lightly removing excess marinade, dipping in the egg mix, followed by the whey protein mix, immediately placing in the hot oil and basting the top right away.

7. You want to fry the fish right after coating for best crispness. Fry on both sides until deep golden and transfer to a paper-lined plate for a few minutes.

8. Serve over a bed of jicama chips, plenty of lemon, mayonnaise and a drizzle of vinegar.

9. Chips: Preheat oven to 400°F.

10. Place jicama slices into a large bowl, add oil, turmeric, garlic powder, onion powder, salt and pepper and toss to coat evenly.

11. Spread the chips onto a baking stone or a baking sheet lined with parchment paper making sure the chips aren't crowded. They need space or else they will start to steam and get soft rather than crispy.

12. Bake for 30 minutes, take them out of the oven and flip, then bake for another 20-30 minutes or until chips are light brown and have reached the desired texture.

13. Remove from oven.

45

INDIAN CAULIFLOWER DISH

Servings: 2

Nutritional Facts Per Serving:
Carbs: 8 g   Protein: 3 g
Fats: 13 g   Calories: 143 kcal

INGREDIENTS

⅓ cup ghee
2 cloves garlic, finely chopped
½ inch ginger, finely chopped
1 tsp coriander seeds
½ tsp cumin seeds
½ tsp brown mustard seeds
½ tsp yellow mustard seeds
½ tsp turmeric, ground
1 cauliflower, processed into rice
2 tbsp cilantro, chopped
salt and pepper to taste

This is how you make the recipe

1. Place the ghee into a large non-stick frying pan over medium-high heat.

2. Add the garlic and ginger and saute until fragrant.

3. Now add the whole spices and saute for 3-5 minutes, until making "popping" noises.

4. Add half of the cauliflower rice and gently mix into the spices and ghee.

5. Saute for 3 minutes before adding the remaining cauliflower rice.

6. Add the pepper and salt to taste.

7. Continue to stir the cauliflower rice while cooking for another 8-10 minutes, until softened and cooked through.

8. Remove the frying pan from the heat and mix through the cilantro.

9. Serve and enjoy.

CURRY PUFFS

Servings: 6			
Nutritional Facts Per Serving:			
Carbs:	5.6 g	Protein:	21.7 g
Fats:	23.1 g	Calories:	315 kcal

INGREDIENTS

Filling:

7 oz ground beef (or ground pork)

½ tsp salt

¼ tsp pepper

1½ tbsp curry powder

1 tbsp sugar-free tomato ketchup

1 cup vegetable broth

½ cup shredded mozzarella

1 tsp lard

Dough:

1½ cups shredded mozzarella cheese

¼ cup cream cheese

1 egg

¾ cup almond flour or 4 tbsp coconut flour

1 tsp aluminum-free baking powder

½ tsp xanthan gum

This is how you make the recipe

1. Filling: In a frying pan, heat one tsp of lard over medium-high heat.

2. Add the meat and cook until browned.

3. Add salt, pepper, curry powder and ketchup. Stir well.

4. Enclose the vegetable broth and simmer for about 20 minutes and let it cool completely.

5. Dough: Preheat the oven to 350˚F.

6. In a large saucepan, melt the mozzarella cheese and cream cheese over low heat until it can be stirred together and remove from the heat.

7. Put an egg into it and stir.

8. Add the almond (or coconut) flour, baking powder and xanthan gum (optional) and mix well.

9. Wet your hand and knead it until it is smooth. Reheat the dough if it gets crumbly. Add flour little by little (½ tsp at a time) if the dough is too sticky.

10. Place the dough on parchment paper. Cover it with another parchment paper and roll it out to rectangle. Cut the dough into six squares.

11. Place the cooked beef and shredded cheese on each square and fold diagonally to form a triangle.

12. Press the edges together

13. Bake for 20-23 minutes or until golden brown.

SCOTCH EGGS

Servings: 6

Nutritional Facts Per Serving:

Carbs:	0.5 g	Protein:	28.2 g
Fats:	22.5 g	Calories:	319 kcal

INGREDIENTS

6 eggs

1 lb ground pork, beef or lamb

2 tsp herbs of choice, optional such as curry, caraway seeds, mustard

1 tsp onion flakes to garnish, optional

salt and pepper to taste

This is how you make the recipe

1. Boil the eggs for four minutes.

2. Mix the ground meat with the herbs, spices and salt.

3. Flatten a small handful of ground meat mix.

4. Place a boiled egg on top and start to mold the meat around the eggs. Add more meat if required to ensure the boiled egg is completely covered.

5. Press firmly to help the meat adhere to the egg.

6. Place on a lined baking tray and brush the Scotch egg with oil and sprinkle on some onion flakes.

7. Bake at 350°F for 15-20 minutes, or until golden on all sides.

8. You can turn the Scotch eggs once while cooking to make sure they are golden all over.

STEAK AND KIDNEY PIE

Servings: 10-12

Nutritional Facts Per Serving:
Carbs:	9.2 g	Protein:	75.6 g
Fats:	26.1 g	Calories:	584 kcal

INGREDIENTS

Filling:

3 lb steak

1½ lb lamb kidney

6 oz portabella mushrooms

1 large sweet onion

1 bay leaf

½ tbsp fish sauce

½ tsp salt, to taste

½ tsp pepper, to taste

3 medium carrots

2 cups beef stock

2 tbsp arrowroot powder

3-4 tbsp bacon grease (or use tallow, lard or coconut oil)

Pastry:

½ cup palm shortening (or substitute unsalted butter)

1 cup full-fat coconut milk

⅓ cup coconut flour, sifted (measure after sifting)

½ cup arrowroot powder

4 eggs + 1 egg yolk

a pinch of of salt

This is how you make the recipe

1. Filling: Slice steak and kidney into quarter inch thick slices. Slice carrot and portabella mushrooms into half inch thick cubes. Slice the onion.

2. Heat 3 tbsp of bacon grease in a large pot over medium high heat. Brown meal and kidney separately in batches. Set aside.

3. Add 1-2 tbsp bacon grease to pan if needed. Brown onion slices, add carrots and mushrooms then cook for 3-4 more minutes.

4. Return meat to the pot. Whisk arrowroot powder into beef stock and add to pot.

5. Add the fish sauce and bay leaf.

6. Simmer and stir uncovered for one and a half hours. Taste and season with salt and pepper as needed.

7. Pour into a large casserole or lasagna dish and let cool to room temperature.

8. Pastry: Combine the flours and salt.

9. Crack your eggs and place them in separate bowls .

10. Preheat oven to 425°F.

11. Heat coconut milk and palm shortening over medium heat until it just starts to simmer.

12. Remove from heat and pour in all of the flour all at once. Stir very well until it's thick and fully combined.

13. Add the eggs one at a time and stir with each addition (you are doing this off the heat). Each time you add an egg, the dough will seem to separate and then as you stir, it will come together. Wait until it comes together before adding the next egg.

14. At the end, you have a fairly warm, quite thick and sticky cream-colored dough.

15. Immediately pour the dough over the cooled steak and kidney filling. Spread with a spoon or spatula to evenly cover the entire surface.

16. Bake for 25-30 minutes, until lightly browned on top (you might want to put a baking sheet under the casserole dish just in case it bubbles over a little).

WELSH CAWL

Servings: 6

Nutritional Facts Per Serving:

Carbs:	13.2 g	Protein:	51.5 g
Fats:	48.7 g	Calories:	698 kcal

Cawl is a simple, traditional Welsh soup. Ideally, eat the Cawl with buttered keto bread and a hunk of strong cheese.

INGREDIENTS

butter or coconut oil

1½ lb bone-in lamb neck, weighed with bone in

salt, pepper

½ a large cauliflower head, cut into florets

2 carrots, cubed

2 radishes, diced

2 small turnips, cleaned (you can leave skin on) and diced

1 small rutabaga, peeled and diced

¼ cabbage head, thinly sliced

thyme or parsley

8½ cups water

This is how you make the recipe

1. Heat a large deep pan on the stove with a little butter or oil. Sprinkle the lamb with a little salt and pepper, then sear in the pan until browned on all sides.

2. Add the water to the pan, and bring to a boil.

3. Lower to a simmer and add all vegetables.

4. Simmer uncovered for 2-3 hours, or till the meat is so tender it falls apart.

5. When the Cawl is ready, take out the meat and shred it, taking care to discard all the bones.

6. Return the meat to the soup.

7. Sprinkle with fresh thyme or parsley and serve in deep bowls.

8. Serve with keto bread, butter and a hunk of strong cheese.

SIDE DISHES

YORKSHIRE PUDDING

Servings: 12

Nutritional Facts Per Serving:

Carbs:	3 g	Protein:	1.3 g
Fats:	1 g	Calories:	27 kcal

INGREDIENTS

3 medium eggs

1⅓ cup arrowroot flour

1½ almond flour

1 cup whole milk

¼ tsp salt

raw coconut oil

This is how you make the recipe

1. Whisk eggs and salt until frothy.

2. Add sifted flours a bit at a time while you whisk.

3. Add milk, little by little.

4. When your batter mix is nice and smooth cover with cling film and set aside for 30 minutes.

5. Pre-heat oven to 340°F .

6. Spread some coconut oil all around your muffin molds and drop half a tsp at the bottom of each; Pace the muffin tray in the oven to warm up.

7. Give your batter a final whisk and pour your Yorkshire pudding batter in, filling each mold slightly less than halfway up.

8. Bake for 30 minutes, then lower the oven temperature to 285°F, open the oven door slightly and continue to bake for 15 more minutes.

9. Turn the oven off, and leave the puddings in to dry and crisp up further.

10. Serve hot or cold.

ENGLISH MUFFIN

Servings: 1			
Nutritional Facts Per Serving:			
Carbs:	8 g	Protein:	12 g
Fats:	27 g	Calories:	307 kcal

INGREDIENTS

3 tbsp blanched almond flour
½ tbsp coconut flour
1 tbsp butter, ghee or coconut oil
1 large egg
½ tsp baking powder
a pinch of salt

This is how you make the recipe

1. Melt the butter (or ghee or oil) in an oven-safe ramekin.

2. Add the remaining ingredients and stir until well combined. Let sit for a minute to allow the mixture to thicken.

3. Bake for about 15 minutes at 350°F.

4. Run a knife along the edge and flip over a plate to release. Slice in half, then toast in the toaster.

CAULIFLOWER COLCANNON

Servings: 4			
Nutritional Facts Per Serving:			
Carbs:	4 g	Protein:	3 g
Fats:	15 g	Calories:	159 kcal

Colcannon is an Irish dish comprised of mashed potatoes with either cabbage or kale. This cauliflower colcannon recipe is a low carbs version of the Irish side dish as it uses cauliflower in place of the traditional mashed potato.

INGREDIENTS

4 cups kale or cabbage, stalk removed and chopped
1 large head of cauliflower, chopped
6 spring onions, finely sliced
one small bunch of chives, finely sliced
⅓ cup almond milk
2 tbsp vegan spread or coconut oil
salt, pepper, nutmeg to taste

This is how you make the recipe

1. Bring a pot of lightly salted water to a boil, add the kale and cook for 10-15 minutes until tender.

2. Boil water and add the cauliflower in a separate pot for 15 minutes until tender.

3. Add the spring onions, chives and milk to a saucepan and simmer for 5 minutes.

4. After the kale is cooked and well drained, drain the cauliflower, remove any excess moisture and mash well. You can use a food processor or immersion blender to puree the cauliflower if you wish.

5. Stir in the kale, milk with spring onions and chives, half of the butter and some salt, pepper, nutmeg.

6. Serve warm with the rest of the butter melting on top. Perfect accompanied with some sausages!

CAULIFLOWER BAKE

Servings: 4

Nutritional Facts Per Serving:

Carbs:	3 g	Protein:	16 g
Fats:	27 g	Calories:	322 kcal

INGREDIENTS

1 whole cauliflower

4 cups shredded mozzarella cheese

½ cup aged cheddar, grated

1 cup sour cream

7 oz bacon rashers

½ onion sliced

1 tbsp Italian herbs

1 garlic

This is how you make the recipe

1. Preheat oven to 350°F.

2. Break the cauliflower up into florets and blanch for 5 minutes until cauliflower is slightly softened. Boil, then quickly run under cold water and drain.

3. In a saucepan melt butter and add garlic, let it cook for about 1 minute.

4. Add the sour cream to a simmer, add cream cheese, mozzarella, until the sauce begins to thicken.

5. Coat the cauliflower with it evenly.

6. Cut the bacon rashers into strips and add on top.

7. Add the onion.

8. Salt, pepper and Italian herbs to taste.

9. Add the grated cheddar.

10. Bake in the oven for 25 minutes.

11. Cover with foil and bake for 30 minutes or until cauliflower is fork tender and the cheese has melted.

CAULIFLOWER CHICKEN SOUP

Servings: 6

Nutritional Facts Per Serving:
Carbs: 8 g   Protein: 16 g
Fats: 45 g   Calories: 490 kcal

INGREDIENTS

3 chicken thighs

21 oz heavy cream

1 cup chicken stock

1 cauliflower cut into florets

5 oz feta cheese, crumbled

2 oz butter

2 cloves garlic crushed

1 tbsp coconut oil

zest of 1 lemon

juice of 1 lemon

1 tbsp dried oregano

1 small diced red onion

½ tsp salt

½ tsp pepper

salt and nutmeg to taste

2 tbsp fresh mint, finely chopped

This is how you make the recipe

1. Preheat oven to 390°F.

2. Place the chicken thighs into a roasting tray and sprinkle over the oil, zest from the lemon and salt.

3. Roast them for 15-20 minutes until browned and cooked through.

4. Dice or shred into small pieces and set aside.

5. Add the butter, oregano, onion and garlic into a large saucepan and saute until the onion is translucent.

6. Add the cauliflower and stir well. Saute for 2 minutes.

7. Include the heavy cream and chicken stock and reduce the heat to a simmer.

8. Let it simmer for 15-20 minutes until the cauliflower is tender.

9. Carefully blend the cauliflower with your immersion blender until there are no lumps remaining.

10. Add the diced chicken, pepper and juice from the lemon and stir well.

11. Crumble the feta cheese into the soup.

12. Add salt and nutmeg if desired.

13. Ladle into bowls and sprinkle over with mint to serve.

CHEESE AND BACON CAULIFLOWER SOUP

Servings: 6

Nutritional Facts Per Serving:

Carbs:	7 g	Protein:	13 g
Fats:	38 g	Calories:	421 kcal

INGREDIENTS

1 head of cauliflower, cut into evenly sized florets

10 oz heavy cream

7 oz bacon, thinly sliced

2 cups chicken stock

1 oz butter

2 cloves garlic, crushed

1 tsp pepper

salt and nutmeg to taste

⅔ cup parmesan cheese, shaved

This is how you make the recipe

1. Place a large saucepan over medium-high heat.

2. Add the butter and garlic and saute for 3 minutes.

3. Add the cauliflower and stir to coat in the butter. Saute for 2 minutes.

4. Add the heavy cream, chicken stock, and pepper, and reduce the heat until the pot is simmering. Simmer for 15-20 minutes, until the cauliflower is tender.

5. While the cauliflower is cooking, prepare the bacon;

6. In a frying pan add the bacon and place over medium-high heat. Saute for 10-15 minutes, until the bacon is starting to crisp.

7. Set the bacon aside, while you blend the cauliflower soup into a smooth puree.

8. Add the bacon and parmesan cheese into the cauliflower soup.

9. Add salt, pepper, nutmeg.

10. Ladle into bowls and serve.

TEA TIME

BISCOTTI

Servings: 12

Nutritional Facts Per Serving:
Carbs:	2.1 g	Protein:	5 g
Fats:	17.6 g	Calories:	187 kcal

When making these biscotti, keep the wet and dry ingredients separate, and then always pour the wet on top of the dry. This biscotti recipe is so easy that you can mix the dough by hand, no food processor needed.
Make sure you allow these biscotti to cool before you slice them for the second bake, otherwise they will fall apart. Also make sure you wait for the biscotti to cool down before you drizzle with the keto chocolate sauce, this will ensure the glaze doesn't melt into the biscotti.

INGREDIENTS

Biscotti:
2 tbsp flax seed
6 tbsp water
2 cups almond flour, sifted for best results
½ cup sunflower seeds, ground into a flour
1 tsp baking powder
⅓ cup pecans or walnuts, chopped
zest of 1 lemon
zest of 1 orange
3 tbsp Swerve
¼ cup coconut oil or grass fed butter
1 tsp pure almond extract
anise to taste

Chocolate drizzle:
2 tbsp finely chopped or shaved baking chocolate
4 tbsp Swerve
1½ tbsp coconut oil

This is how you make the recipe

1. Preheat oven to 300°F. with the oven rack set in the middle.

2. Prepare the flax egg by mixing the flax meal and water in a small bowl and allow to sit at least 15 minutes so it can thicken.

3. Put the almond flour in a large bowl.

4. Use a coffee grinder or food processor to turn the sunflower seeds into flour. Add the ground sunflower seeds, baking powder, lemon and orange zest, pecans, and mix well with a whisk.

5. Pour the flax seed egg mixture into a separate bowl and add the Swerve, almond extract, coconut oil, and mix well.

6. Add the wet batter on top of the dry batter and mix well until the dough comes together. Use your hands to mix once the dough firms up.

7. Place a piece of parchment paper on a baking tray and with your hands, form the dough into a 10 x 3 inch log. You can make the shape wider and shorter if desired.

8. Bake for 35 minutes then remove from oven and allow cool down for 15 minutes.

9. Once cooled, use a sharp knife to cut the log into ¾ inch wide biscotti pieces and lay them on a cooling rack.

10. Place the cooling rack on to the sheet and bake for another 25-30 minutes until the biscotti are golden brown and have color around the edges. If you don't have a cooling rack, flip the biscotti halfway to ensure even baking on each side.

11. Melt the chocolate. (approx 125°F).

12. Add the Swerve and coconut oil, and whisk until the sauce is smooth and creamy. If it is a bit grainy or cools down before drizzling, continue heating until smooth.

13. Remove biscotti from oven and allow to cool for 10 minutes before drizzling with chocolate sauce.

ALMOND BISCOTTI

Servings: 12

Nutritional Facts Per Serving:

Carbs:	3.2 g	Protein:	3.6 g
Fats:	9.7 g	Calories:	108 kcal

INGREDIENTS

2 cups almond flour

1 cup whole raw almonds, skin on

2 large eggs, beaten

½ cup Swerve

1 tsp sugar-free vanilla extract

1 tsp baking powder

1 tsp xanthan gum

½ tsp nutmeg

¼ cup butter, melted

This is how you make the recipe

1. Pre-heat oven to 320°F.

2. Mix dry ingredients: almond flour, Swerve, baking powder, xanthan gum, spices and almonds together in large bowl.

3. Melt the butter and add it and the beaten eggs into mixture. Mix well until a dough forms.

4. Line a baking tray with parchment paper. Form the dough into a low, wide log shape.

5. Since the dough is a bit sticky, you should dust your hands with coconut flour.

6. Bake for approx. 45 minutes or until loaf is browned on the outside and firm in the center

7. Remove from oven and let cool fully to room temperature.

8. Once cold, cut the loaf into slices about ½ inch thick.

9. If your loaf is refusing to slice and is very crumbly, I recommend allowing it to sit out overnight and go slightly stale. This will not affect the finished quality, but will greatly enhance the slice-ability of the loaf.

10. Pre-heat oven to 250°F. Lay the slices in a flat layer on one or two lined baking trays. Toast for 15-20 minutes each side.

RASPBERRY EARL GREY TEA COOKIES

Servings: 10			
Nutritional Facts Per Serving:			
Carbs:	1.3 g	Protein:	2.5 g
Fats:	8 g	Calories:	88 kcal

These raspberry Earl Grey tea cookies are a tasty way to get a lift in the afternoon.

INGREDIENTS

1 cup raw walnuts

2 tbsp Earl Grey black tea

2 tbsp Swerve

1 tbsp sugar-free raspberry syrup

1 tsp raspberry extract

1 egg

½ tsp baking soda

This is how you make the recipe

1. Preheat oven to 375°F.

2. Grind the tea into a fine powder.

3. Grind the nuts in a food processor until it becomes a batter but not yet a smooth nut butter.

4. Spoon into a mixing bowl, add the rest of your ingredients and mix well.

5. Cover a cookie sheet with parchment paper.

6. Spoon out batter, about a tbsp each.

7. Bake for 8 minutes. Check to make sure they are nice and brown but not too crunchy.

8. Serve with your favorite afternoon tea.

9. Store in a sealed container.

SCONES

Servings: 6

Nutritional Facts Per Serving:
Carbs: 3 g Protein: 4 g
Fats: 12 g Calories: 137 kcal

INGREDIENTS

1½ cups almond flour
2 large eggs
4 tbsp unsalted butter
1 tbsp baking powder
⅓ cup sour cream
strawberry chia seed jam
whipped heavy cream
butter
coconut oil

This is how you make the recipe

1. Preheat the oven to 395°F.

2. Grease a 12 cup muffin tray with coconut oil.

3. Melt the butter and let it cool.

4. In a large bowl, combine the dry ingredients and combine evenly.

5. Once the butter has cooled, add the eggs and sour cream and stir to combine.

6. Add the wet ingredients to the dry ingredients and mix thoroughly until everything is evenly combined.

7. Scoop heaped tbsp of the batter into the muffin pans

8. Bake for 10-12 minutes until the tops are golden brown.

9. Serve with butter, jam and cream and a cup of tea.

DESSERTS

SUMMER FRUITS ENGLISH TRIFLE

Servings: 6

Nutritional Facts Per Serving:

Carbs:	6 g	Protein:	10 g
Fats:	55 g	Calories:	568 kcal

INGREDIENTS

Simple sponge:

1 cup ricotta

⅓ cup Swerve

3 eggs

3½ oz butter, melted

¾ cup almond flour

1 tsp baking powder

½ tsp salt

Trifle:

10 oz simple sponge

2 cups double cream (heavy cream)

2 egg yolks

1 tsp vanilla paste or 1 vanilla bean

1¼ tbsp Swerve

½ sheet gelatin

5 oz frozen summer fruits

⅛ cup almonds

½ packet of strawberry jelly powder

This is how you make the recipe

1. Sponge: Preheat oven to 340°F.

2. Using an electric mixer, beat the ricotta and Swerve together.

3. While mixing, add in eggs, one at a time.

4. Add melted butter, almond flour, baking soda and salt.

5. Pour mixture into a 8 x 12 inch baking dish (use parchment paper) and bake for 30-40 minutes until the skewer stays dry.

6. Trifle: Cut up thin slices of sponge and line the bottom of 6 dessert bowls.

7. Lay frozen fruits over the sponge in each bowl, pressing them down into the sponge.

8. Dissolve ½ packet of strawberry jelly powder in 5 oz of boiling water and then add 5 oz cold water to make the jelly.

9. Stir well, pour jelly over fruit and sponge in each bowl.

10. Place in the refrigerator to set while you prepare the custard.

11. Put yolks and Swerve in a medium bowl, whisk until frothy.

12. Fill a cup with cold water and immerse ½ sheet of gelatin; set aside to soften.

13. In a saucepan, combine 1¼ cups cream with vanilla; bring to just below simmering.

14. Remove cream from heat and add it, one ladle at a time, to the egg yolk mix, whisking vigorously.

15. Take the egg-cream mix to the saucepan, add the softened gelatin (after squeezing excess water out if it) and place on low heat, whisking continuously until it thickens.

16. Transfer the custard to a heat-proof bowl, cover with cling film and leave to cool down.

17. Take the bowls of jelly-fruit/sponge out of the refrigerator and add a layer of cooled custard. Put the bowls back in the refrigerator to set.

18. Whip ¾ cup double cream and spoon it into your 6 bowls.

19. Roast almonds for 5 minutes and crush them.

20. Sprinkle them over the top of each bowl and serve.

CHOCOLATE BROWNIE TRIFLE

Servings: 8

Nutritional Facts Per Serving:

Carbs:	37.3 g	Protein:	8.5 g
Fats:	36 g	Calories:	377 kcal

INGREDIENTS

Brownies:

3½ oz dark chocolate

7 oz of unsalted butter

1 cup Swerve

1 tsp of vanilla

a pinch of salt

4 eggs

1 cup almond flour

Mousse:

3½ oz dark chocolate, broken into pieces

2 tbsp heavy cream

½ cup mascarpone cheese

1 cup heavy cream, whipped

This is how you make the recipe

1. Brownies: Melt the chocolate and butter together.

2. Whisk in a quarter of a cup of Swerve, 1 tsp of vanilla, a pinch of salt and 4 eggs, one at a time.

3. Then add in almond flour and bake it in a well-greased baking dish in the oven at 350°F for 20 to 25 minutes.

4. Once the brownies have cooked and cooled, you can make your chocolate mousse.

5. Mousse: Melt the chocolate and 2 tbsp cream over low heat.

6. Once melted, remove from the heat and pour into a bowl.

7. Whisk the mascarpone into the chocolate mixture, until smooth.

8. In a separate bowl, whip the cream until thickened peaks are formed.

9. Once the cream is whipped, fold it gently through the chocolate mixture until smooth.

10. Divide the mousse into portions and place into the refrigerator for a few hours to set.

CHRISTMAS TRIFLE

Servings: 12

Nutritional Facts Per Serving:

Carbs:	4 g	Protein:	6 g
Fats:	35 g	Calories:	374 kcal

INGREDIENTS

Sponge Cake:

1 cup ricotta

⅓ cup Swerve

3 eggs

3½ oz butter, melted

¾ cup almond flour

1 tsp baking powder

½ tsp salt

Trifle:

4 packets sugar-free port wine jelly crystals

2½ cups water

2 cups heavy cream

1 cup fresh raspberries

1 cup fresh strawberries

1¼ cups thickened cream

This is how you make the recipe

1. Sponge: Preheat oven to 340˚F.

2. Using an electric mixer, beat the ricotta and Swerve together.

3. while mixing, add in eggs, 1 at a time.

4. Add melted butter, almond flour, baking soda and salt

5. Pour mixture into a 9 inch by 9 inch baking dish.

6. Bake for 30 minutes.

7. Trifle: Place jelly crystals in a heatproof bowl. Add boiling water. Stir to dissolve crystals. Stir in 1⅔ cups cold water.

8. Refrigerate overnight.

9. Cut the sponge into 2 inch square pieces. Arrange sponge in a 13 cup capacity serving bowl.

10. Spoon half the jelly over top. Top with heavy cream.

11. Sprinkle with raspberries and strawberries.

12. Spoon remaining jelly over top.

13. Refrigerate, covered, overnight.

14. Using an electric mixer, beat thickened cream and Swerve in a bowl until soft peaks form.

15. Spoon mixture over trifle. Top with raspberries and strawberry quarters.

COFFEE AND ALMOND SYLLABUB

Servings: 4		
Nutritional Facts Per Serving:		
Carbs:	16.6 g	Protein:	1.2 g
Fats:	10.3 g	Calories:	106 kcal

INGREDIENTS

8 dry roasted unsalted almonds, roughly chopped

2 tsp ground coffee

1 cup whipping cream

¼ cup confectioners Swerve

½ tsp almond extract

¼ cup unsweetened almond milk

This is how you make the recipe

1. Heat the almond milk in a small pan and add the coffee. Stir until dissolved then set aside to cool off.

2. Pour the confectioners Swerve, the cold coffee mixture, the almond extract and the cream into the bowl of a stand mixer.

3. Using a whisk attachment, whisk the ingredients together on a high speed for a few minutes until the cream begins to thicken. Once it has begun to thicken, reduce the speed and continue to whisk until thick and fluffy peaks form on the surface.

4. Divide the mixture evenly between four serving glasses.

5. Scatter the almonds over the syllabub to serve.

GINGERBREAD LOAF

Servings: 10

Nutritional Facts Per Serving:

Carbs:	4 g	Protein:	6 g
Fats:	26 g	Calories:	275 kcal

INGREDIENTS

Bread:

1½ cup of almond flour
4 oz of cream cheese, softened
1 large egg
½ cup of butter, softened
½ cup of Swerve
2 tsp of ginger, ground
1½ tsp of baking powder
1 tsp of cinnamon, ground
½ tsp of vanilla extract
½ tsp of cloves, ground
½ tsp of nutmeg, ground
a pinch of salt

Frosting:

4 oz of cream cheese, softened
1 tsp of vanilla extract
¼ cup of walnuts, roughly chopped

This is how you make the recipe

1. Bread: Preheat oven to 330˚F.

2. Add the butter and Swerve to your stand mixer and cream on medium speed using the whisk attachment.

3. Add the vanilla, egg and cream cheese and combine.

4. In a mixing bowl, add the remaining loaf ingredients and mix together.

5. Then fold the dry ingredients into the stand mixer.

6. Pour the batter into a 9 x 5 inch loaf pan, lined with parchment paper.

7. Bake for 50-55 minutes, until a skewer comes out clean when inserted in the center.

8. Allow the loaf to sit in the pan for 15 minutes before removing to a wire cake rack to cool completely.

9. Frosting: In your stand mixer, combine the cream cheese, vanilla and Swerve. Mix on medium speed until smooth.

10. Spread over the cooled loaf and top with the chopped walnuts.

11. Cut into 10 slices and enjoy.

MOCK APPLE PIE

Servings: 6

Nutritional Facts Per Serving:

Carbs:	6.6 g	Protein:	2 g
Fats:	16.7 g	Calories:	187 kcal

The mock apple pie, made from crackers, was probably invented for use aboard ships, as it was known to the British Royal Navy as early as 1812.

INGREDIENTS

Crust:
2 sticks of unsalted butter
4 large eggs
1½ cups coconut flour
2 tsp of Swerve
½ tsp salt

Filling:
5 chayote squash
¾ cup of Swerve
¼ cup of lemon juice
2 tbsp of cinnamon powder
2 tbsp of butter, sliced thinly
½ tsp of salt

This is how you make the recipe

1. Crust: Melt the butter and allow to cool. Set aside.

2. In a large mixing bowl combine the coconut flour, Swerve, and salt.

3. To the dry ingredients add the cooled melted butter and 4 eggs.

4. Mix all the ingredients just until dough forms.

5. Divide dough in half to make the top and bottom of the pie crust.

6. Roll out each dough half between two sheets of parchment paper. Set aside.

7. Transfer one crust into a 8 inch pie pan. Being careful to smooth out any cracks.

8. Note the pie crust will be fragile but the dough easily comes together by pressing it.

9. Filling: Boil the chayotes whole, peel and slice.

10. Cook the chayote slices 15 to 20 minutes until tender.

11. Place the slices in a large bowl and add the Swerve, lemon juice, salt and cinnamon powder. Combine well.

12. Pour the chayote mixture into the prepared pie crust.

13. Dot the top of the filling with slices of butter.

14. Top the pie with the other pie crust.

15. Press the edges around the pie with the tines of a fork to seal the two crusts together. Cut slits on pie to allow to vent.

16. Bake the pie for 35-40 minutes at 375˚F.

93

LEMON CUSTARD TARTS

Servings: 2

Nutritional Facts Per Serving:

Carbs:	8 g	Protein:	17 g
Fats:	95 g	Calories:	963 kcal

INGREDIENTS

Crust:

3 tbsp melted butter

¾ cup almond meal

½ tsp dried lavender flowers
(optional)

Filling:

4 large egg yolks

zest of 3 lemons

½ cup melted butter, unsalted

½ cup fresh lemon juice

¼-½ cup sugar-free vanilla syrup

This is how you make the recipe

1. Preheat oven to 375°F.

2. Grease two 10 oz ramekins.

3. With mortar and pestle, grind lavender flowers into a fine dust.

4. Mix lavender, almond flour, and 3 tbsp melted butter.

5. Press mix into the bottom of the dishes.

6. Bake for 10 minutes or until the tops begin to brown, then remove from the oven.

7. In a blender or food processor, blend the egg yolks, lemon zest, lemon juice, vanilla syrup and ½ cup melted butter until smooth.

8. Transfer filling to a small saucepan and cook over medium-low heat, stirring constantly with a spatula for about 15 minutes until thick like pudding.

9. Pour the filling over the almond-lavender crust in the two dishes.

RHUBARB POSSET

Servings: 4

Nutritional Facts Per Serving:

Carbs:	3.2 g	Protein:	2.1 g
Fats:	21.6 g	Calories:	223 kcal

INGREDIENTS

1½ cup diced rhubarb

6 oz double cream (heavy cream)

¾ cup regular Swerve

¼ confectioners Swerve

1 tbsp ground cinnamon

½ tsp water

½ cup ground ginger

½ tsp vanilla extract

This is how you make the recipe

1. Place the diced rhubarb to a small pan with the water with the ¾ cup of regular Swerve. Bring the mixture to a boil and stir to combine, then reduce to a simmer for 3-5 minutes, until the rhubarb is soft.

2. Strain the water from the rhubarb and mash the fruit lightly with a fork. Set aside to cool.

3. Add the confectioners Swerve, whipping cream, cinnamon, ginger and vanilla to the bowl of a stand mixer.

4. Using a whisk attachment, whisk on a high-speed setting until the cream begins to thicken, this may take a couple of minutes. As it starts to thicken, reduce the speed and continue to whisk, forming thick and fluffy peaks.

5. Divide the mashed rhubarb mixture in half and carefully fold one half through the whipped cream.

6. With the remaining half, add a heaped tsp to the base of a ramekin or serving glass.

7. Divide the cream and rhubarb mixture evenly between the 4 serving vessels and then top each with the remaining rhubarb.

8. Serve immediately.

LAVA CAKE PUDDING

Servings: 2

Nutritional Facts Per Serving:

Carbs:	8 g	Protein:	9 g
Fats:	15 g	Calories:	192 kcal

Butter. Not quite an ingredient, but it is rather essential. Firstly, butter the heck out of it. Otherwise your cake might stick. Even more importantly, don't be afraid to take this cake out of the oven when it's still super-jiggly. Eat these cakes straight out of the oven! If you leave them in the ramekins too long, they will continue to cook and set more than you might like.

INGREDIENTS

4 tbsp cocoa powder

2 eggs

3 tbsp heavy whipping cream

3 tbsp Swerve

1 tbsp vanilla extract

½ tsp baking powder

butter

This is how you make the recipe

1. Preheat oven to 350°F.

2. In a bowl combine the dry ingredients: cocoa powder, Swerve, baking powder.

3. In a separate bowl beat the eggs well. Add the heavy whipping cream, vanilla extract and mix again.

4. Add the egg mixture to the dry ingredients and combine until you get a pour-able consistency.

5. Grease 2 ramekins with some butter.

6. Bake for 12 minutes or until the top is set but still moist. Be careful not to over-bake them.

7. Turn out onto plates and serve hot!

STRAWBERRY RHUBARB CRUMBLE

Servings: 6

Nutritional Facts Per Serving:

Carbs:	8.7 g	Protein:	4.2 g
Fats:	20.6 g	Calories:	230 kcal

INGREDIENTS

Filling:

1 cup strawberries, finely diced

1 cup rhubarb, finely diced

1 tbsp lemon juice

1 tsp Swerve

½ tsp xanthan gum

Crumble:

1 cup walnuts, finely chopped

½ cup coconut flour

¼ cup flax-seed meal

¼ cup Swerve

6 tbsp unsalted butter, melted

¼ tsp sea salt

This is how you make the recipe

1. Preheat oven to 350°F.

2. In a bowl, combine the filling ingredients. Sprinkle the xanthan gum in gently so that it's evenly spread and doesn't clump.

3. In another bowl, combine the crumble ingredients: walnuts, coconut flour, flax-seed meal, ¼ cup Swerve, salt and mix evenly.

4. Add butter to the crumble and combine until the whole mix is crumbly.

5. Set ½ cup of the crumble aside and add the remaining ½ tsp Swerve to it.

6. Grease a pie dish with butter, then press down the bowl of crumble. Use your hands to press it flat into the bottom.

7. Pour the fruit mixture over the crust and spread evenly.

8. Finally, sprinkle the remaining ½ cup of crumble over the pie.

9. Bake for about 20 minutes covered with tinfoil, then a final 10-20 minutes until crumble is browned.

10. Once finished, let cool down in the refrigerator

VICTORIA SANDWICH CAKE

Servings: 6

Nutritional Facts Per Serving:

Carbs:	3.6 g	Protein:	6.1 g
Fats:	22.1 g	Calories:	237 kcal

INGREDIENTS

Cake:

4 eggs, room temperature

5 oz Swerve

1¼ cup almond flour

1 tsp baking powder

1 tbsp pure vanilla extract

2 oz butter, softened

¼ tsp salt

½ cup cream cheese

Filling:

1 cup double cream (heavy cream)

2 tbsp confectioners Swerve

¾ cup raspberry balsamic chia jam

This is how you make the recipe

1. Preheat the oven to 350°F.

2. Using a stand mixer, beat the Swerve with the softened butter, until fluffy.

3. Add softened cream cheese and beat until combined.

4. With the mixer add the eggs one at a time, beating it well in between each egg. Add vanilla.

5. In a bowl, place almond flour, baking powder and salt and mix until combined.

6. Grease and line one large (9 inch) or six individual (4.5 inch) spring-form pans.

7. Pour batter into pans and bake for 45-60 minutes. Check the cakes after 45 minutes. Small cakes will take less time to cook than one large cake.

8. Remove from oven. Let it cool.

9. Once cool, remove from pan and cut in half.

10. Place cream and additional Swerve into bowl and whisk until firmly whipped.

11. Spread a layer of raspberry balsamic jam on to one side of the cake.

12. Spread a layer of whipped cream on the other side and sandwich together.

13. Dust with confectioners Swerve, if desired.

14. You can store it in the refrigerator for two days.

Go to **www.ketoveo.com** for more guides and resources to help
you on your keto journey.

Made in the USA
Las Vegas, NV
09 July 2021